15
FAT QUARTER
MAKES

Edited by Ame Verso

**FIFTEEN SEWING PROJECTS
MADE USING FAT QUARTERS**

----INTRODUCTION----

Every crafter just loves to stash fabric – especially fat quarters – and is always on the lookout for new ideas to quilt, stitch and appliqué. 15 Fat Quarter Makes, is overflowing with exciting and inspirational projects for all those lovely fabric bundles: the ones you already have stored away and those you are yet to buy!

So what exactly is a fat quarter? Taken from one yard or metre of fabric, fat quarters are cut in half lengthways and then in half widthways to form a quarter cut, (usually) measuring 18 × 22in (45× 56cm), but often a slightly larger 20 × 22in (50 × 56cm). Widely available pre-cut in an array of patterns and colours; their squarer shape makes them highly versatile for patchwork, appliqué, strip piecing and more, which is why crafters adore them so much. This unique collection begins with single fat quarter patterns for everyday items, such as purses and sunglasses cases, that can be completed in less than a day. You can then move onto more complex projects requiring a small handful of fat quarters: from a fun girly twirly skirt to a lovely sewing machine cover and even a handy fabric basket to brighten up your home. If you are feeling ambitious, why not savour the stunning projects that use up to 10 fat quarters? They will bust your much-loved fabric stash and give you family heirlooms to treasure, including striking pillows and beautiful quilts that will take you from winter through to summer. The handy side bar on every page will tell you at a glance how many fat quarters you will need for each project – just look for the shaded diamonds.

So be inspired, release that fabric stash and get creative with these easy-to-follow patterns, complete with a handy stitch library to get you started. Everything you need in one beautiful package to make a wealth of useful and stylish projects for your home, garden, family and friends.

----CHIC SUNGLASSES CASE----

Ali Burdon

This stylish case, sewn from a single fat quarter, is perfect for protecting your summer shades. The button and loop fastening gives you easy access to your eyewear and you can mix and match your styles by experimenting with different fabrics and trims.

MATERIALS

◆ 1 fat quarter of fabric

◆ 10in (25cm) medium loft fusible fleece

◆ 10in (25cm) medium weight iron-on interfacing

◆ 2in (5cm) length of ribbon, lace or trim

◆ 3in (7.5cm) length of elastic cord

◆ ¾in (2cm) diameter button

◆ PATTERN NOTES

Seam allowance is ¼in (6mm)

1 Cut four pieces from the fat quarter (two for the outer and two for the lining), two pieces from the fusible fleece and two pieces from the interfacing, each measuring 6 × 8in (15 × 20cm). Iron the fusible fleece to the outer fabric and the interfacing to the lining fabric, following the manufacturer's instructions.

2 Fold the trim or ribbon in half and pin, right sides together, to the right-hand edge of the outer front, 2¾in (7cm) from the top. The raw edges of the ribbon should just overlap the right-hand raw edge of the fabric.

3 Place the second piece of outer fabric right sides together with the first, sandwiching the folded ribbon in-between. Pin and stitch the sides and bottom seam. Pin the lining fabrics, right sides together, then stitch the side and bottom seams, leaving a 3in (7.5cm) opening in the centre of

the bottom seam for turning.

4 To create the flat base, draw a 1in (2.5cm) square at each bottom corner of the lining section. Open out the pouch and pinch one of the corners, bringing the side and bottom seams together. Match the markings and then stitch along the line created, reverse stitching at both ends. Repeat for the other corner. Trim the excess fabric at the corners, leaving a ¼in (6mm) seam allowance, then turn right sides out and iron. Repeat for the outer section pieces.

5 Mark the mid-point of the lining on the top edge of the back section. Fold the elastic cord in half and tack (baste) the loop within the seam allowance at this point on the right side of the lining. The raw edges of the loop should just overlap the raw edge of the lining, and the loop itself should point towards the lower seam.

6 Turn the outer section right sides out and place it into the lining section, right sides together. The loop should be sandwiched between the lining and the outer, with just the raw edges showing. Line up the side seams, pin around the top edge and stitch.

7 Turn the pouch through the opening. Iron the top seam and topstitch it close to the edge. Fold the top down and stitch the button in place. Finally, ladder stitch the gap in the lining closed.

----CHARMING COIN PURSE----

Kaye Prince

Featuring a strong faux leather base panel and zip fastening, this coin purse is both pretty and practical. As it uses just one fat quarter, there is nothing stopping you from making a variety of purses in different colourways to complement your every look.

MATERIALS

- 1 fat quarter of fabric
- 1 fat quarter of medium weight interfacing
- Small piece of faux leather
- 7in (18cm) zip

◆ PATTERN NOTES

Seam allowance is ½in (1.2cm)

Top Tip

FOR NEAT ZIP CORNERS, FOLD THE TABS TOWARDS THE OUTER PIECES AND THE SEAMS TOWARDS THE LINING PIECES.

1 Cut four 5 × 6in (13 × 15cm) rectangles (two for the outer and two for the lining) and two 1¼ × 2½in (3 × 6.5cm) rectangles (for zip tabs) from the fat quarter. Cut a ¾ × 2½in (2 × 6.5cm) and two 6 × 1½in (15 × 4cm) rectangles from the faux leather and two 5 × 6in (13 × 15cm) rectangles from the interfacing.

2 Fuse the interfacing to the outer pieces, following the manufacturer's instructions. Align a leather piece along the bottom edge of an outer piece and topstitch along the top edge of the leather. Repeat for the other outer piece.

3 Evenly trim the zip to 5½in (14cm). Take one zip tab piece, iron each short edge in towards the wrong side by ¼in (6mm) and fold in half widthways. Repeat. Fit the zip end inside the tab, butting the end up against the fold, and topstitch in place across the ironed edge. Repeat at the other end of the zip with the second tab.

4 Centre and place the zip, face down, along the top edge of the right side of one outer panel. Place one lining panel right side down on top and pin. Stitch through all three layers using your zipper foot. Turn the panel right side out so the lining and outer pieces are wrong sides together and iron. Repeat with the second outer piece, placing it right side up and laying the sewn piece on top with the zip face down. Topstitch the fabric together along each zip edge.

5 Fold the small leather rectangle in half widthways. Press and align the raw edges along one side of an outer piece, about 1in (2.5cm) from the zip. Tack (baste) in place.

6 Open the zip at least three-quarters of the way and fold the purse so both lining and outer pieces are aligned right sides together. Stitch around the purse, leaving a turning gap in the bottom of the lining. Turn right sides out, using a wooden stick or similar to push out the corners. Stitch the opening closed and iron.

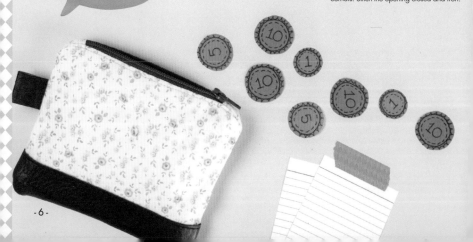

-6-

----CURIOUS CAT DOORSTOP----

Lisa Fordham

This charming doorstop is simple to sew from just two fat quarters using the templates provided. The addition of a filled beanbag inside the body makes the doorstop fully functional, as well as adding bags of character to your home.

MATERIALS

- ◆ 2 fat quarters of fabric
- ◆ 1kg (2lb 4oz) of dried beans
- ◆ 2 small black buttons
- ◆ Toy stuffing

◆ PATTERN NOTES

Seam allowance is ⅛in (4mm)

1 Using the templates provided (see Templates) cut the following from the two fat quarters: one bottom panel, two body pieces (on the fold), two head pieces, four ears, four paws, two tails and two beanbag pieces.

2 With right sides facing, machine stitch two ear shapes together, leaving a turning gap, and turn right sides out. Lightly stuff with toy stuffing, fold in by ⅛in (4mm) and hand stitch the gap closed. Repeat for the other ear, the tail and the two paws.

3 With right sides facing, pin and mark areas on the head to be left open for the ears and neck. Leave a 2¼in (5.5cm) opening for each ear, with a 2¾in (7cm) gap between them. Machine stitch the head pieces together around the openings and turn the head right sides out. Place the stuffed ears into each opening and hand stitch them in position on both sides. Lightly stuff the head with stuffing, being careful not to overfill, then hand stitch the opening in the neck closed.

4 Stitch the two body pieces right sides together along the curved edge then stitch the bottom panel to the base of one body piece, right sides facing. Stitch the bottom panel to the base of the other body piece, leaving a large gap for stuffing and inserting the beanbag.

5 Machine stitch the two beanbag pieces together, leaving a small gap. Insert the beans through the opening then machine stitch it closed. Fill the body with stuffing, inserting the beanbag last, then add just a small amount of stuffing to finish. Fold down the small seam around the bottom piece and hand stitch in place.

6 Stitch claw lines onto the paws with black wool and stitch the paws and tail in position. Make the face by attaching two black buttons for the eyes and embroidering a nose and whiskers using black wool. Finally, stitch the head to the front of the body.

Ali Burdon

This versatile vintage-style basket made from three fat quarters is so useful for extra storage in the kitchen. Use it to hold small packets or eggs, or fill it with fruit as a pretty fabric alternative to a fruit bowl.

MATERIALS

◆ 3 fat quarters of fabric: main, lining and edging

◆ 10in (25cm) flexi-firm fusible interfacing

◆ 10in (25cm) medium loft fusible fleece

◆ 10in (25cm) medium weight fusible interfacing

◆ PATTERN NOTES

Seam allowance is ¼in (6mm)

1 Cut a 9in (23cm) diameter circle and two 3 × 14in (7.5 × 35cm) rectangles from the main fabric and lining fabric. Cut four 2 × 14in (5 × 35cm) rectangles from the edging fabric.

2 Cut a 9in (23cm) diameter circle and a 4½ × 27½in (11.5 × 70cm) rectangle from flexi-firm fusible interfacing, medium loft fusible fleece and medium weight fusible interfacing.

3 Take one of the 3 × 14in (7.5 × 35cm) main fabric pieces and pin one of the edging pieces to the top edge, right sides together. Stitch then iron the seam open. Repeat for the other main fabric and lining pieces.

4 To add a decorative fabric tab to the side of your basket (optional), cut a 3 × 2½in (7.5 × 6.5cm) piece from your desired fabric. Make a crease down the centre, parallel with the 2.5in (6.5cm) edges, fold the edges into the middle crease, then fold along the crease. Iron then stitch closed, near to the edge, and then topstitch the folded edge to match. Fold in half again to create the tab. Pin the folded tab to one of the outer sections, right sides together, with the raw edges of the tab aligned with one of the short sides. Position about 1¾in (4.5cm) from the top edge.

5 Pin the two outer sections, right sides together, and stitch down one short edge (sandwiching the tab). Iron the seam open and the tab endings to one side. Repeat for the two lining pieces.

6 Fuse the flexi-firm interfacing to the wrong side of the outer section, then fuse the fusible fleece on top of the interfacing, following the manufacturer's instructions. Fuse the circular piece of flexi-firm interfacing to the main fabric circle, then fuse the fusible fleece on top.

7 Fuse the medium weight interfacing to the wrong side of the lining sides and base circle.

8 On the outer section, topstitch the edging fabric close to the seam between the main and edging fabric.

9 Pin then stitch the other short edges of the outer sections, wrong sides together, to create a tube. Repeat with the lining section.

10 Mark the quarter points on the outer circular base and the outer side. Pin the base to the side section, right sides together, pinning the marked points together first, then the gaps in-between. Stitch the base to the sides. When you need to stop to pivot the fabric, leave the needle down to stay on the seam line. Iron this seam well to get a neat finish, then repeat for the lining sides and base.

11 Turn the outer section right side out and slip it inside the lining section, right sides together. Make sure the two bases are snug against each other and the side seams line up. Stitch around the top edge, leaving a 4–5in (10–12.5cm) turning gap, and reverse stitch at either end of the seam.

12 Turn the basket through the opening. Iron thoroughly, turning in the raw edge on the turning gap as you iron. Pin or glue the gap closed using a washable glue stick, then topstitch the top edge of the basket. Fasten off the ends to finish.

----ELEGANT E-READER CASE----

Kaye Prince

This simple-to-sew case is designed to fit a 7in (18cm) tablet or e-reader. As well as looking chic, it is handy for protecting your tablets from scratches and knocks while you're on the go.

MATERIALS

◆ 3 fat quarters of fabric
◆ 1 fat quarter of medium weight interfacing
◆ 1 fat quarter of quilt wadding (batting)
◆ ¾in (2cm) button

◆ PATTERN NOTES

Seam allowance is ½in (1.2cm)

1 From the first fat quarter cut two 6½ × 9½in (16.5 × 24cm) rectangles for the outer panels and two 6 × 4½in (15 × 11.5cm) rectangles for the flap.

2 From the second fat quarter cut one 6½ × 7½in (16.5 × 19cm) rectangle for the outer pocket.

3 From the third fat quarter cut two 6½ × 9½in (16.5 × 24cm) rectangles for lining, one 6½ × 7½in (16.5 × 19cm) rectangle for pocket lining, and one 1¼ × 4in (3 × 10cm) rectangle for the button loop.

4 From medium weight interfacing cut a 6½ × 7½in (16.5 × 19cm) and a 6 × 4½in (15 × 11.5cm) rectangle. Cut two 6½ × 9½in (16.5 × 24cm) rectangles from quilt wadding.

5 Layer one outer panel with one quilt wadding panel, pin together and tack (baste). Quilt with vertical lines ½in (1.2cm) apart. Trim the quilted panel down to 6½ × 9½in (16.5 × 24cm) if necessary. Repeat with the other outer and wadding panels.

6 Fuse the 6½ × 7½in (16.5 × 19cm) piece of interfacing to the outer pocket rectangle. Place the outer pocket and pocket lining pieces right sides together and sew along one short side. Turn right side out so the wrong sides are together, iron and topstitch along the seamed edge. Sew the button to the pocket, 2in (5cm) from topstitched edge.

7 Fold the button loop piece in half lengthways with right sides together and sew along one long edge. Turn right side out, iron, and topstitch along the two long sides. Fuse the second interfacing piece to one flap rectangle. Loop the button loop piece and with the raw edges aligned tack to the flap piece. Place both flap pieces right sides together and stitch around one long and two short sides. Turn right sides out, iron, and topstitch along the three seamed edges.

8 Line up the pocket piece on top of one outer panel and tack in place. Place the outer pieces right sides together and sew along the bottom and sides. Turn right side out and iron. With the raw edges aligned, match the flap piece along the back top edge of the case and tack in place.

9 Place the lining pieces wrong sides together and sew along the bottom and sides, leaving a turning gap in the bottom. Place the outer pouch inside the lining, so the right sides touch, and stitch around the top edge. Turn right side out using the turning gap, then iron and sew the gap in the lining closed. Finally, topstitch along the pouch opening.

Top Tip

YOU CAN MAKE A SMALLER VERSION OF THE E-READER CASE TO FIT YOUR SMART PHONE.

Cynthia Shaffer

I love the fun theme of this farmyard print fabric, which is beautifully complemented by the bold green tree and pocket appliqué details. What better way to protect your sewing machine, while keeping it looking fresh and vibrant at your workstation?

MATERIALS

- ◆ 3 fat quarters of print fabric: 2 brown, 1 green
- ◆ 9in (23cm) square of fusible web

1 Using the brown print fabric, cut two 7 × 5½in (18 × 14cm) panels. With right sides facing, stitch the panels together with a ½in (1.2cm) seam allowance, matching the long edges. Iron the seam open.

2 Using the template (see Templates), trace the tree onto the paper side of the fusible web. Cut out approximately ½in (1.2cm) from the traced edge. Place the web side down onto the wrong side of the green print fabric and fuse, following the manufacturer's instructions. Cut out the tree and peel off the paper backing. Place the green tree on the brown stitched fabric, 3in (7.5cm) from the bottom and left side and fuse in place.

3 Stitch around the tree in off-white perle cotton using long running stitches and an occasional overcast stitch.

4 Cut a 5¼in (13.5cm) square pocket from the green print fabric. Iron the top edge under by 1in (2.5cm) then stitch in place.

5 Trace the pocket panel (see Templates) onto the paper side of the fusible web, cut out and fuse to the brown fabric, as in Step 2. Centre the brown pocket panel 1½in (4cm) from the bottom of the pocket and fuse, as before. Repeat Step 3 to stitch around the panel.

6 Iron the sides and the bottom edge of the pocket under by ½in (1.2cm). Pin to the sewing machine cover, 3½in (9cm) up from the bottom and right side, and stitch in place.

7 Cut five 1½ × 20in (4 × 50cm) strips from green fabric. Stitch the short ends together to make a 1½ × 100in (4 × 250cm) strip. Iron in half widthways then iron the edges into the ironed fold to create a binding strip.

8 Stitch the binding around the outer edge of the cover. Now sew running stitches around the binding using off-white perle cotton.

9 Cut four 2 × 13in (5 × 32cm) green fabric strips. Iron in half widthways, iron the edges into the fold and stitch the strip together. Stitch these strips to the inside of all four sides of the cover, 5½in (14cm) from the bottom edges.

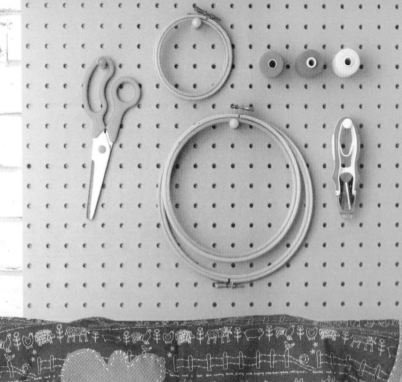

Prudence Rogers

This little floral bear is so sweet on her own, but she wouldn't be seen without her miniature dress. It only takes two fat quarters, but you can have fun using up fabric scraps to make her a whole wardrobe!

MATERIALS

◆ 2 fat quarters of fabric: main teddy and dress
◆ 28in (71cm) length of ¼in (6mm) wide ribbon
◆ Toy stuffing

Top Tip

THE HEM IS A LITTLE TRICKY TO SEW, DUE TO THE SIZE OF THE DRESS. IT HELPS TO TURN THE DRESS TO RIGHT SIDES, WHILE STILL SEWING THE HEM FROM THE WRONG SIDE.

1 Using the template (see Templates), cut out two teddy shapes from the main fabric (seam allowance is included).

2 Place the teddy bear's right sides facing and sew around, using a ¼in (6mm) seam allowance and leaving a 2in (5cm) turning gap down the outer side of one leg.

3 Cut into the corners and clip all the curves on the seam allowance. Turn to right sides through the opening and iron.

4 Sew ¼in (6mm) from the edge around each ear through both thicknesses of fabric (see Fig 1).

5 Stuff the teddy with toy stuffing through the opening in the leg. Fold the raw edges of the opening under to match the seams and slipstitch closed by hand.

6 Hand sew the eyes, nose and mouth using satin stitch and backstitch in a contrasting colour, as shown in the photograph.

7 Cut two dress shapes (see Templates) from the second fat quarter. With wrong sides up, fold over each armhole by ¼in (6mm) around the curve and iron. Don't worry if the

seam allowance becomes smaller as the turn tightens. Stitch the folded edge around each armhole closed (see Fig 2).

8 Fold the top neckline down by ¼in (6mm), then a further ⅜in (1cm) to conceal the raw edge, then iron and pin. Sew close to the bottom folded edge to make a casing for the ribbon. Repeat for the other dress piece.

9 With right sides facing, pin the front and back dress pieces together. Sew down each straight side using a ¼in (6mm) seam allowance. Finish the seam with zigzag stitch and fold to one side (see Fig 3).

10 Fold and iron a ⅜in (1cm) hem around the bottom of the dress and sew ¼in (6mm) from the folded edge.

11 Thread a 14in (35.5cm) length of ribbon through each casing, using a small safety pin at one end. Centre the ribbon and sew a small vertical row of stitching in the middle of the casing. Heat-seal the ends of the ribbon to prevent them from fraying. Place the teddy in the dress, pull up the ribbons to gather the top and tie in a bow at each side.

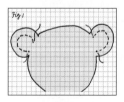

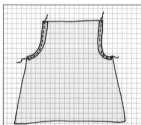

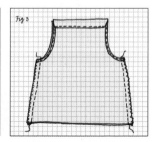

CRAFTER'S TREASURE BUCKET

Cynthia Shaffer

Every crafter will have a stash of their favourite yarns, fabrics, needles, hooks and pins. Now these treasured items can be stored together in this must-have bucket – complete with sturdy base, strap and generous side pockets – all crafted from four stylish fat quarters.

MATERIALS

- ◆ 4 fat quarters of fabric: 1 for outer, 1 for lining, 2 for pockets
- ◆ 18in (46cm) fusible pellon
- ◆ 18in (46cm) heavyweight fusible interfacing
- ◆ 1in (2.5cm) silver overall buckle
- ◆ 36in (91.5cm) white cotton strapping, 1in (2.5cm) wide
- ◆ 2yd (1.8m) length of white double-wide seam binding

◆ PATTERN NOTES

Seam allowance is ½in (1.2cm)

1 Cut a 22 × 12½in (55 × 32cm) and an 8½ × 12½in (22 × 32cm) panel from the fat quarter of the outer fabric. Stitch the panels together, right sides facing, along the 12½in (32cm) edges and iron the seams flat.

2 Place the panel from Step 1 on top of the fusible pellon and cut around. Fuse the pellon to the wrong side of the panel, following the manufacturer's instructions.

3 Repeat Steps 1 and 2 for the lining fabric.

4 Using the template (see Templates) cut out two pockets from one of the pocket fabrics, two pockets from the other pocket fabric and four pockets from the heavyweight fusible interfacing. Following the manufacturer's instructions, fuse the interfacing to the wrong side of the pocket pieces. Bind the top edges (with the convex curves) with white binding.

5 Pin the pockets to the bottom edge of the outer bucket panel, alternating the fabric patterns. Pin the first pocket 1¼in (3cm) from the left edge, aligning the bottom edges. Pin the right pocket edge parallel to the left pocket edge. The pocket will bulge out away from the panel.

6 Position the next pocket 1¾in (4.5cm) from the first, aligning the bottom edges, and pin the edges in place. Repeat for the two remaining pockets, placing the last one 1¼in (3cm) from the right side of the bucket panel. Sew the pockets in place; stitching down one side, pivoting at the bottom and stitching up the remaining side. Reverse stitch at the start and end of your sewing.

7 With right sides facing, stitch the side seam of the bucket. Repeat for the lining and iron the seams. Slip the lining with right sides out into the outer bucket with wrong sides out, matching the top edges and side seams. Pin in place and stitch together. Turn the bucket so the lining is on the outside, pin the layers together at the bottom and stay stitch them in place.

8 To make the base, draw two 9¼in (23.5cm) diameter circles on the leftover fabric and one on the fusible pellon, either using a pair of compasses or a pencil tied to a piece of string. Fuse the pellon to the wrong side of one of the base pieces. Layer the other bottom piece on top of the pellon, pin the layers and stay stitch together. Pin the base to the outer bucket and stitch the layers together.

9 Using the remaining white binding, bind off the base and bucket seam. Flip the bucket right sides out.

10 Iron and then stitch around the top edge, ¼in (6mm) away from the top. Fold the top down by 1½in (4cm) and iron into place.

11 To make the strap cut a 1¼ × 36in (3.5 × 91.5cm) strip of fabric – you will need to piece this together to get the length. Iron the edges under by ¼in (6mm), centre the strip onto the cotton strapping and stitch into place.

12 Slip the strap into one of the pockets, 6½in (16.5cm) from the folded top edge. Pin and then stitch in place. Slip the overall buckle onto the opposite end of the cotton strap. Following the manufacturer's instructions set the overall button through all the layers, exactly opposite to where the strap goes into the pocket. Hook the overall buckle onto the overall button and adjust the strap as desired.

----COOL COLOURBLOCK TOTE----

Kaye Prince

Shop in style with this bright tote bag sewn from panels of bold block colour, complete with a sturdy handle and handy interior pocket. Have fun choosing colours to suit your style and quilting in your own design to make a totally unique tote!

MATERIALS

◆ 6 fat quarters of fabric
◆ 18in (46cm) fusible fleece
◆ 9in (23cm) medium weight interfacing

◆ PATTERN NOTES

Seam allowance is ½in (1.2cm)

1 For the tote outer and interior pocket cut two 8 × 20in (20 × 50cm) rectangles from fat quarter 1 and two 9 × 20in (23 × 50cm) rectangles from fat quarter 2. From fat quarter 3 cut two 4 × 20in (10 × 50cm) rectangles and one 10 × 15in (25 × 38cm) rectangle for the pocket.

2 For the tote lining and handles cut two 8 × 20in (20 × 50cm) rectangles from fat quarter 4, two 9 × 20in (23 × 50cm) rectangles from fat quarter 5 and four 4 × 20in (10 × 50cm) rectangles (two for the handles) from fat quarter 6.

3 Cut two 19 × 20in (48 × 50cm) rectangles from the fusible fleece and two 3½ × 20in (9 × 50cm) rectangles from the interfacing.

4 To piece the outer and lining panels, line up one 8 × 20in (20 × 50cm) rectangle, one 9 × 20in (23 × 50cm) rectangle, and one 4 × 20in (10 × 50cm) rectangle along their long sides. This is the layout for each tote panel: sew these three rectangles together

to form the panel. Repeat for all four panels (outer and lining).

5 To make the interior pocket, fold the 10 × 15in (25 × 38cm) rectangle in half, right sides together, to form a 10 × 7½in (25 × 19cm) rectangle. Sew along the three open sides, leaving a turning gap in the long side. Turn to the right side, using a wooden stick or similar to push out the corners, then iron. Topstitch along the long folded edge.

6 Centre the pocket and topstitch it to one of the finished lining panels, topstitching the turning hole closed at the same time. Run another line of stitching down the centre of the pocket to divide it into two compartments.

7 Fuse fusible fleece to each outer tote panel following the manufacturer's instructions, then quilt the outer panels, as desired.

8 Place the outer panels right sides together and sew along the bottom and sides. Repeat for the lining panels, leaving a 4–5in (10–13cm) opening in the bottom.

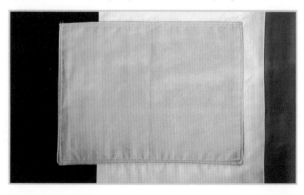

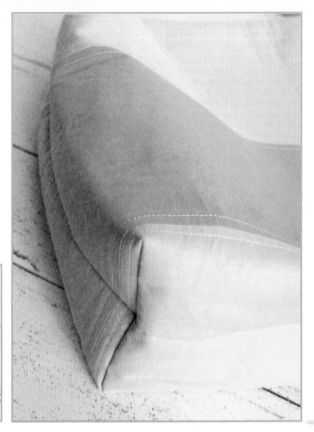

9 To form the boxed corners, take the outer tote piece (wrong sides out) and match the side and bottom seams at one corner. Hold flat, centre the seam, and measure 2½in (6.5cm) up from the point. Draw a line across from side to side. Sew along the line and trim the seam to ½in (1.2cm). Repeat with the other corner and both corners of the lining.

10 To make the handles, fuse the interfacing to each 4 × 20in (10 × 50cm) handle rectangle, then fold them in half lengthways with right sides together. Sew along the open long sides and turn each handle right side

out. Iron and topstitch along each long side and then again ¼in (6mm) away from each long edge. Loop each handle over and centre on the tote so the raw edges are aligned (the loops should be pointing down). The inner edges of each handle loop should be spaced 4in (10cm) apart. Tack (baste) in place.

11 Turn the outer tote piece right side out and place inside the lining piece, right sides together. Align the side seams and pin, then sew along the top edge. Turn the tote right side out through the opening in the lining and stitch the turning gap closed. Finally, iron the top edge and topstitch around.

----QUILTED OVEN MITT----

Jessie Fincham

This practical oven mitt will make an attractive addition to your kitchen accessories. The coordinating binding, hanging loop and crosshatch quilting detail give this cooking essential a professional finishing touch.

MATERIALS

- ◆ 3 fat quarters of fabric: inner, outer and binding
- ◆ 20in (50cm) wadding (batting)

1 Sandwich the wadding (batting) between the inner and outer fabric and pin to secure.

2 Using the template provided (see Templates), draw a mitt shape onto the sandwiched layers of fabric, then turn the template over and draw an opposite mitt shape. Cut a rough rectangle around each mitt, leaving 1in (2.5cm) around the edge.

3 Quilt straight lines with a 1in (2.5cm) spacing to create a diagonal or crosshatch effect (see Fig 1). Repeat for the other mitt, then cut out the mitt shapes.

4 Fold the binding fabric in half diagonally and trim off the excess to make a square. Cut one 2in (5cm) strip along the diagonal to create bias binding. Iron the binding in half lengthways, open up again and iron the raw edges to the centre ironed line.

5 Sew the binding to the bottom outside edge of each mitt panel, leaving a few inches for

a 'tail' at the start and finish. Iron the binding strips and mark a pencil line at both ends, in line with the mitt ends. Sew along these lines and trim off the excess. Fold over the opposite side of the binding and hand or machine sew.

6 Make a hanging loop by trimming off an 8in (20cm) length of binding. Fold in half lengthways and sew very close to the edge. Fold in half to create a loop and pin to the outer side of the mitt.

7 Place both mitt pieces right sides together and sew around the edge with a ¼in (6mm) seam allowance, using a walking foot to feed through the thick layers. Sew the hanging loop in place at the same time. Zigzag stitch around the edge and trim off any excess. Turn the mitt right sides out, pushing out the edges with a wooden stick or similar.

Top Tip

WHEN DRAWING AROUND THE TEMPLATES, MAKE SURE YOU LEAVE ENOUGH SPACE BETWEEN EACH SHAPE AND THE EDGES OF THE FABRIC.

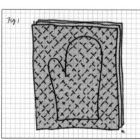

----COUNTRY CONTRAST PILLOW----

Jessie Fincham

This 15in (38cm) square pillow is the perfect addition to a country cosy living room or bedroom. The half square triangles (HST) that form the pattern are so simple to make. Play with the contrast of colour and pattern within each square for striking results.

MATERIALS

◆ 7 fat quarters of fabric: 5 for pillow top (plain beige, blue check, cream floral, plain green, purple floral), 2 for pillow back

1 Cut two 3in (7.5cm) strips from the width of fabric from the beige, check and cream fat quarters, then sub-cut each fabric into nine 3in (7.5cm) squares. Cut one 3in (7.5cm) strip from the width of fabric from the green and purple fat quarters, then subcut each fabric into five 3in (7.5cm) squares.

2 To make a half square triangle (HST) place two 3in (7.5cm) squares right sides together. Draw a pencil mark through the diagonal and sew ¼in (6mm) from each side of the drawn line. Cut down the centre line to yield two HST units and iron towards the darker side.

3 Repeat with 18 squares, using your chosen fabric placement, to yield a total of 36 completed HST units.

4 Join the pillow top in rows, carefully matching the correct fabric placement. Iron the seams to the side, alternating with each row so the seams can 'nest' together. Sew the blocks together as shown and iron the seams open.

5 Cut two 15½ x 11½in (39.5 x 29cm) pieces from the backing fabric. Fold the shorter side over by 1in (2.5cm) and again by 1in (2.5cm), enclosing the raw edge, and iron. Sew ⅛in (3mm) from the folded edge. Repeat for the other side.

6 With right sides together, place the pillow top with the pillow sides on top of each other. Pin and sew ¼in (6mm) around the edge. Cut the corners and trim off the excess with pinking shears.

----CHEVRON QUILT----

Emily Levey

This fun quilt is surprisingly simple to make using one simple half square triangle (HST) block that is repeated throughout. It is the clever light and dark print selection that forms the striking chevron pattern.

MATERIALS

- 10 fat quarters of fabric: 5 light prints, 5 dark prints
- 20in (50cm) length of 44in (110cm) wide cotton fabric for binding
- 48 × 64in (122 × 163cm) quilter's wadding (batting)
- 50 × 66in (127 × 168cm) backing of your choice

◆ PATTERN NOTES

Seam allowance is ¼in (6mm), unless stated otherwise

Top Tip

FOUR OF THE REMAINING FIVE HST UNITS CAN BE SAVED TO MAKE A COORDINATING CUSHION.

1 Cut four 9¾in (24.5cm) squares from each fat quarter.

2 On the reverse of each light print square use a fabric marker to draw a diagonal line from one corner to the other. Pair each light print square with a dark print square. With right sides facing, sew two lines of stitching on either side of the diagonal line, ¼in (6mm) away from it. Cut down the line to give you two units and iron the seam allowances towards the dark print.

3 Repeat Step 2 until you have sewn all the squares together and have 40 HST units.

4 Trim each of the HST units so that they are 9in (23cm) square, taking care to ensure that the seam line runs diagonally from one corner to another.

5 Arrange the HST units to form the chevrons, using 35 units in a layout of five columns by seven rows (see Fig 1). With right sides facing, stitch the squares together until each row is sewn. Iron the seam allowances on each row in opposite directions.

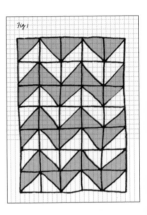

Fig 1

6 Place the first two rows together, right sides facing. Align the seams: they should lock together with the seam allowances facing in opposite directions, and sew. Repeat until all rows are joined and iron the seam allowances open to reduce bulk.

7 With the wrong side facing up, lay your backing out smoothly on a large solid surface, securing it in place with masking tape at the corners if needed. Take care not to stretch the backing out of shape.

8 Lay the wadding out smoothly on top of the backing. Place the completed quilt top on top so

the right side is facing up, ensuring that there is an even overlap of wadding/backing fabric all the way around. Pin through all the layers with safety pins, spacing the pins about 4in (10cm) apart around the quilt.

9 Quilt as desired. Here a straight stitch with a ⅛in (3.5mm) stitch length has been used to echo the zigzag lines of the chevrons. Remove the safely pins as necessary while quilting, then trim the excess backing and wadding once the quilting is complete.

10 Take your binding fabric and cut five 2½in (6.5cm) × width of fabric strips. Join the strips along the short ends so you have a long length. Iron the seam allowances open, then iron the binding in half lengthways to make a double fold binding. You will need your binding to be at least 6yd (5.5m) long.

11 On the front of the quilt and starting along the middle of one edge, leave around 6in (15cm) of the binding unsewn, and attach the binding to the quilt with a ¼in (6mm) seam allowance. Align the raw edges of the binding with the edge of the quilt. Mitre the corners as you go and stop sewing around 6in (15cm) from where you started.

12 Mark where the start of the binding tape overlaps with the tail end, then add on ¼in (6mm) for seam allowance and trim both ends. Join the short ends together using the ¼in (6mm) seam allowance, then finish attaching the binding to the quilt along the unsewn section. Hand stitch the binding to the reverse of the quilt to finish.

----DOUBLE-SIDED STAR PILLOW----

Kaye Prince

This large, comfortable floor pillow features a striking star pattern made up from half square triangles in plain and patterned fabrics. Turn the cushion over for a repeat of the design in an alternative colourway, or leave this side plain for a quicker make.

MATERIALS

- ◆ 10 fat quarters of fabric: 8 print, 2 solid
- ◆ 1¾yd (1.6m) quilt wadding (batting)

◆ PATTERN NOTES

Seam allowance is ¼in (6mm)

1 Cut four 6in (15cm) squares each from one print and one solid fat quarter. Cut four 5½in (14cm) squares from print fabric and two 6in (15cm) squares from solid fabric. Now cut one 6in (15cm) square and six 5½in (14cm) squares each from two print fat quarters and eight 5½in (14cm) squares from one print fat quarter.

2 Repeat Step 1 for the five fat quarters that make up the reverse of the pillow. Then cut two 30in (75cm) squares from quilt wadding.

3 Make the half square triangles by matching up all 6in (15cm) squares in pairs of one solid and one print square. Draw a diagonal line from corner to corner on the back of one square, then match squares with right sides together and pin. Sew a line ¼in (6mm) from each side of the drawn line. Cut the square in half along the drawn line and iron each half open. If necessary, trim the square down to 5½in (14cm). Repeat for each 6in (15cm) square.

4 Lay out all the half square triangles and remaining squares, as shown in Fig 1. Sew all the squares together in each row then sew the rows together.

At each corner, trim the corner square on the diagonal using the points of the two adjacent squares as a guide.

5 Repeat Steps 3 and 4 for the reverse side of the pillow.

6 Place one piece on top of the wadding and trim the wadding down to match the outline of the pillow. Repeat with the reverse of the pillow.

7 Tack (baste) each pillow piece to its respective wadding piece. If desired, quilt each pillow piece. Match the pillow pieces, right sides together, and sew along all sides using a ½in (1.2cm) seam, leaving a turning gap. Turn the pillow right sides out, using a wooden stick or similar to push out the corners. Stuff to the desired firmness and hand sew the turning gap closed.

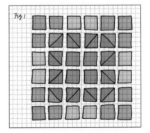

Fig 1

---SNUGGLE SOFT PLAYMAT----

Emily Levey

This adorable quilt playmat, featuring fun fabric prints and colourful ties, is ideal for baby's playtime. Use any backing of your choice: here I have chosen supersoft fleece for a soft and comfortable finish, perfect for snuggling beneath.

MATERIALS

- ◆ 6 fat quarters of fabric
- ◆ 37 × 54in (94 × 138cm) backing of your choice

◆ PATTERN NOTES

Seam allowance is ¼in (6mm),

unless stated otherwise

Top Tip

IF YOU ARE USING FLEECE BACKING, MAKE SURE THE IRON IS NOT TOO HOT WHEN PRESSING THE SEAMS.

Top Tip

TAKE CARE NOT TO STRETCH THE BACKING OUT OF SHAPE, PARTICULARLY IF YOU ARE USING FLEECE.

1 Cut nine 6in (15cm) squares from each fat quarter.

2 Lay out the 54 squares in your desired arrangement of six columns by nine rows. With right sides facing, stitch the squares in each row together. Iron the seam allowances on each row in opposite directions

3 Place the first two rows together with right sides facing. Align the seams, so they lock together with the seam allowances facing in opposite directions and sew, using a walking foot if you have one. Repeat until all rows are joined, then iron the seam allowances.

4 With the right side facing up, place the backing smoothly out onto a large, solid surface, securing the corners in place with masking tape if needed.

5 Place the completed quilt top down on the backing, right sides facing, ensuring there is an even overlap of backing fabric all the way around. Pin the layers together along all four edges.

6 Starting in the middle of one side, sew around with a ⅝in (1.5cm) seam allowance, stopping about 10in (25cm) short of the starting point to leave a turning gap. Reverse stitch at the start and end to secure the stitches.

7 Trim the bulk from the corners and excess backing and turn the quilt the right sides out. Push out the corners and gently iron along the seams to ensure they sit on the very edges of the

quilt. Fold in the unsewn raw edges of the opening and iron, then pin together.

8 Topstitch around the quilt, ¼in (6mm) from the edge, to close up the opening.

9 Thread the needle with coordinating embroidery cotton and insert it through both layers of the playmat, coming back up ¼in (6mm) away. Leave a 2–3in (5–7.5cm) tail then repeat the stitch in the same location, this time pulling the thread taught.

10 Cut the thread, leaving another 2–3in (5–7.5cm) tail, then tie the two tails together with a double knot. Trim the tails to your desired length: around 1in (2.5cm) is best.

11 Repeat Steps 9–10 over the rest of the playmat using embroidery cotton in different colours; this one is tied at the corner of every block.

----GIRLY TWIRLY SKIRT----

Emily Levey

This gorgeous gathered skirt features an elasticated waistband for comfort, and a contrasting hem band for style. By cutting the elastic to size, the skirt can be made to fit girls of three to six years. A larger skirt can be sewn for an older child by increasing the size of the contrasting hem band, however it will not be as full.

MATERIALS

- ◆ 2 fat quarters of fabric: main and accent
- ◆ ¾in (2cm) wide elastic, cut to child's measurements

◆ PATTERN NOTES

Seam allowance is ⅝in (1.5cm)

1 Cut selvedges of the same size from the fat quarters. Cut your main print fat quarter in half along the length, as shown (see Fig 1).

2 With right sides facing, join the two halves along the short edge to give you a 10 × 44in (25 × 112cm) rectangle. Finish the seam allowance and iron.

3 Cut two rectangles from the accent fabric measuring 5½in (14cm) × width of fabric (see Fig 2).

4 With right sides facing, join the two halves along the short edge to form a 5½ × 44in (14 × 112cm) rectangle. Finish the seam allowance and iron.

5 With right sides facing, join the two skirt panels along the long edge (see Fig 3), finish the seam and iron downwards. If you are using a directional print, ensure the accent fabric is sewn along the bottom edge.

6 Join the sides of the skirt to form a tube, finish the seam and iron. Ensure the seam on the hem band matches up on each side.

7 Turn over the top edge of the skirt by ¼in (6mm), bringing the raw edge over to the wrong side of the fabric, and iron. Now turn over by 1in (2.5cm), enclosing the raw edge, and iron again. Stitch around the top of the skirt, ⅞in (2.2cm) from the top edge, to catch this fold. Leave a 2in (5cm) gap for inserting the elastic.

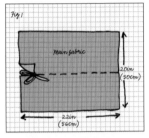

Fig 1
Main fabric
20in (50cm)
2.2in (56cm)

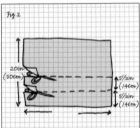

Fig 2
20in (50cm)
5½in (14cm)
5½in (14cm)

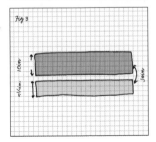

Fig 3
10in
4½in

8 To make the hem turn over the bottom edge by ¼in (6mm), bringing the raw edge over to the wrong side of the fabric, and iron. Turn over again by 1in (2.5cm), enclosing the raw edge, and iron. Stitch around the bottom of the skirt, ⅞in (2.2cm) from the bottom edge.

9 Cut a length of elastic to the child's measurements, using the following as a guide:

3 years = 18¾in (48cm)

4 years = 20in (50cm)

5 years = 21in (53cm)

6 years = 22in (56cm)

10 Using a large safety pin, feed the elastic around the skirt in the top opening, taking care not to twist it. Overlap the ends by 1in (2.5cm) and secure together with a zigzag stitch. Stitch the opening closed.

11 Topstitch around the top of the skirt twice, sewing through the elastic to prevent it from twisting whilst being worn (see Fig 4). Stretch out the elastic as you sew to ensure that the fabric lies flat.

Top Tip

IF THE ELASTIC IS SLACK, A GENTLE STEAM WITH AN IRON ON A HIGH STEAM SETTING WILL HELP IT TO SHRINK BACK. HOLD THE IRON JUST ABOVE THE FABRIC WITHOUT TOUCHING IT.

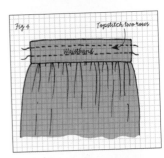

Fig 4   Topstitch two rows

Waistband

----STITCH LIBRARY----

The following stitches feature throughout the projects to add decoration,
for hemming and for closing gaps and seams.

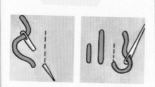

Straight stitch

Straight (long) stitch is worked like a single running stitch: you can make stitches of short or long lengths.

Tacking stitch

Tacking (basting) stitches are used to fasten layers of material together before stitching and can be removed once the stitching is complete. Stitches should be approximately ⅝in (1.5cm) long and evenly spaced.

Running stitch

This simple line stitch can be used to outline shapes or join two pieces of fabric together. Starting at the right-hand side, bring the needle out at A and insert it at B. Bring it out again at C and insert it at D. Continue in this way making sure the stitches and gaps are of even length.

Slip stitch

Slip stitch is used to close gaps in seams. Work from right to left picking up a tiny piece of the fabric from one seam edge. Insert the needle into the other seam fold and move it along by ⅛in (3mm). Push the needle out and repeat.

Whipstitch

Whipstitch (oversewing) is a simple stitch used to sew two pieces of material together. Pull each whipstitch tight for a neat finish.

Backstitch

Backstitch is ideal for making a well-defined outline. Bring the needle out at A and take it to B to make a stitch. Now bring the needle back past the first stitch to C and repeat in this way.

Ladder stitch

Ladder stitch is used to close a seam on a stuffed item or for sewing two folded edges together. Take straight stitches into the folded fabric, stitching into each edge in turn; the stitches look like a ladder. Pull the thread taut after a few stitches to close the seam.

Bullion knots

Bullion knots are worked in a similar way to a French knot, but with more twists around the needle. Insert the needle at B and bring it out at A, without pulling it right through the fabric. Twist the thread around the needle five or six times, so the twists will cover the length between A and B. Place your thumb on the coiled thread and carefully pull the needle through to make the knot.

Cross stitch

Cross stitch is worked to make decorative stitches. Bring the needle out at A and make a diagonal stitch to B. Now bring the needle out at C and make a second diagonal stitch to D. To make a row of cross stitches, bring the needle out at C again and repeat.

Lazy daisy stitch

The lazy daisy stitch is a group of single, detached chain stitches worked in the shape of a flower. Bring the needle up through the fabric at the centre of the flower. Insert it again at the starting point and bring the tip up through the fabric at the opposite end, where the petal will end. Insert the needle back into the fabric on the opposite side of the thread, at the curved

end of the loop, tacking it in place. Repeat to work additional stitches around the centre point.

French knots

French knots can be worked singly as decorative stitches, in rows, or grouped together for a textured filling stitch. To make a French knot, bring the needle and thread through the fabric and wrap the thread around the needle three or four times. Holding this coil of thread in place, take the needle back through the fabric, just next to where it came out.

Sewing machine stitches

FRENCH SEAM

In a French seam, the raw edges of the fabric are fully enclosed for a neat finish. First sew the seam with wrong sides together, then trim and iron the seam allowances. Next sew a second seam with right sides together, enclosing the raw edges of the original seam.

OVERLOCK STITCH

An overlock stitch connects two pieces of fabric with a series of thread loops that wrap around the outer edge of the material to prevent it from fraying. It can be used for hemming, reinforcement or decoration and is sometimes called serging, overedging, or merrowing. True overlock stitching requires an overlock machine, or serger.

STAY STITCH

Stay stitching is a simple row of stitches to help hold the shape of a piece of fabric. It is useful on diagonal cutting lines or curved areas, such as necklines, to prevent stretching. It can also be used for sewing over folds of fabric, such as tucks, to help to hold them in place.

TOPSTITCH

Topstitching is used most often on garment edges, such as necklines and hems, where it helps facings to stay in place and gives a crisp edge. It is generally done using a straight stitch with a matching thread.

ZIGZAG STITCH

A zigzag stitch is a back-and-forth stitch used where a straight stitch will not suffice, such as in reinforcing buttonholes, in stitching stretchable fabrics and in temporarily joining two work pieces edge-to-edge. When creating a zigzag stitch, a cam controls the back-and-forth motion of the sewing machine's needle. As the cam rotates, a finger-like follower connected to the needle bar rides along the cam and tracks its indentations. As the follower moves in and out, the needle bar is moved from side to side.

All templates are shown at 50 per cent; you will need to enlarge them by 150% .
All of the full-sized patterns can be downloaded from http://ideas.stitchcraftcreate.co.uk/patterns

CURIOUS CAT
DOORSTOP

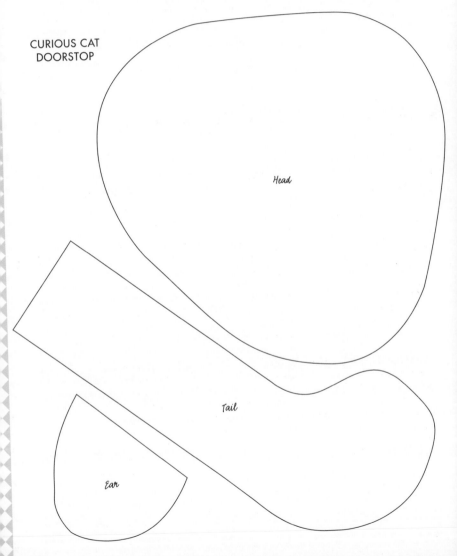

Head

Tail

Ear

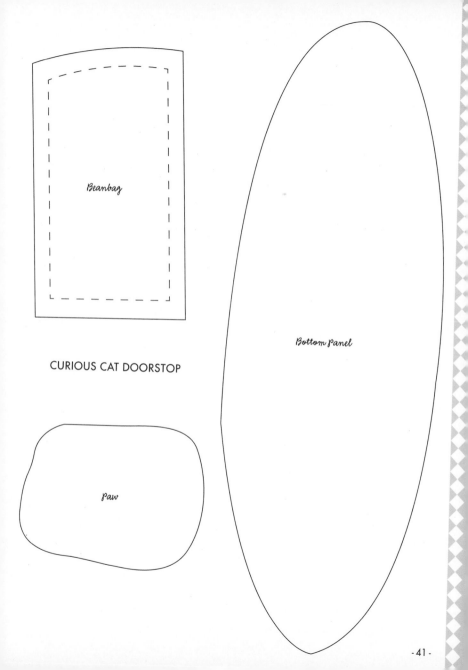

Beanbag

CURIOUS CAT DOORSTOP

Paw

Bottom Panel

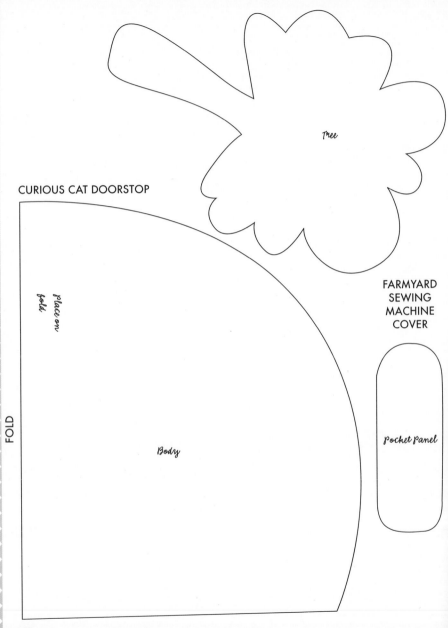

CURIOUS CAT DOORSTOP

Tree

FARMYARD
SEWING
MACHINE
COVER

place on fold

FOLD

Body

Pocket Panel

DITSY TEDDY BEAR

Teddy

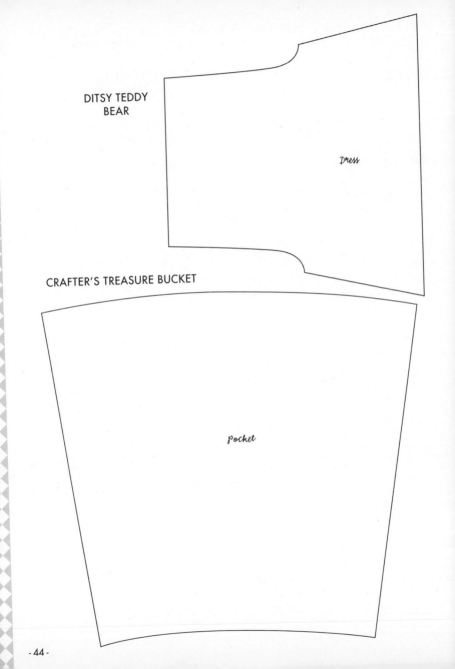

DITSY TEDDY
BEAR

Dress

CRAFTER'S TREASURE BUCKET

Pocket

QUILTED OVEN MITT

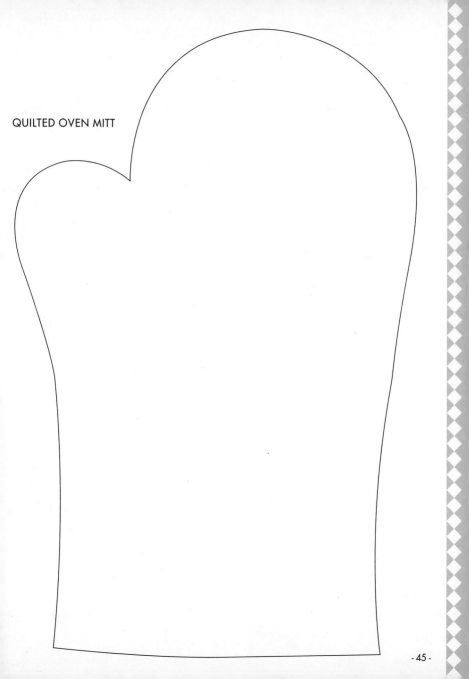

--CONTRIBUTORS--

Jo Avery
www.mybearpaw.com

Ali Burdon
www.veryberryhandmade.co.uk

Jessie Fincham
www.messyjessecrafts.blogspot.co.uk

Lisa Fordham
www.etsy.com/shop/twinciehandmade

Emily Levey
www.strawberrypatchramblings.blogspot.co.uk

Kaye Prince
www.kayeprince.com

Prudence Rogers
www.instagram.com/PrudenceSays

Cynthia Shaffer
www.cynthiashaffer.typepad.com

The publishers would like to thank all of the contributors whose designs have been featured in this book.

A DAVID & CHARLES BOOK
© F&W Media International, Ltd 2015

David & Charles is an imprint of F&W Media International, Ltd
Brunel House, Forde Close, Newton Abbot, TQ12 4PU, UK

F&W Media International, Ltd is a subsidiary of F+W Media, Inc
10151 Carver Road, Suite #200, Blue Ash, OH 45242, USA

Text and Designs © F&W Media International, Ltd 2015
Layout and Photography © F&W Media International, Ltd 2015

First Published in the UK and USA in 2015

The author and publisher have made every effort to ensure that all the
instructions in the book are accurate and safe, and therefore cannot accept
liability for any resulting injury, damage or loss to persons or property,
however it may arise.

Names of manufacturers and product ranges are provided for the information
of readers, with no intention to infringe copyright or trademarks.

A catalogue record for this book is available from the British Library.

ISBN-13: 9780995460614 Paperback

Printed in China by RR Donnelley for:
F&W Media International, Ltd
Brunel House, Forde Close, Newton Abbot, TQ12 4PU, UK

10 9 8 7 6 5 4 3 2 1

Acquisitions Editor: Ame Verso
Editorial Manager: Honor Head
Desk Editor: Debbie Jackson
Project Editor: Bethany Dymond
Designer: Prudence Rogers
Photographer: Jack Kirby
Production Controller: Beverley Richardson

F+W Media publishes high quality books on a wide range of subjects.
For more great book ideas visit: www.stitchcraftcreate.co.uk

Layout of the digital edition of this book may vary depending
on reader hardware and display settings.